SPITTING IMAGES

CREATED BY FLUCK & LAW

PHOTOGRAPHS BY JOHN LAWRENCE JONES

THE WRITERS

PATRICK BARLOW ● CRAIG BROWN ● JULIE BURCHILL ● NIK COHN

RICHARD CURTIS ● PETE DAVIES ● RUSSELL DAVIES ● IAN DURY

FRANCES EDMONDS ● BEN ELTON ● HARRY ENFIELD ● STEPHEN FRY

GERMAINE GREER ● BARRY HUMPHRIES ● MORAY HUNTER &

JOHN DOCHERTY ● TAMA JANOWITZ ● FRANK KEATING

SEAN KELLY ● JOHN LLOYD ● CLIVE MERRISON ● JOHN MORTIMER

TOM NAIRN ● TOM SHARPE ● SUE TOWNSEND ● HUGO VICKERS

JOHN WELLS ● HEATHCOTE WILLIAMS

AND GORE VIDAL

CENTURY London Melbourne Auckland Johannesburg

PRINCE CHARLES

What I want to ask you is this…How would Someone who's the Colonel-in-Chief of fifteen regiments; Someone who has the run of one thousand seven hundred and fifty rooms, with four butlers, six footmen, thirty-six chaplains, fourteen dressers, twenty-six maids, four hundred maintenance staff, ten doctors, eighty dailies, sixty grooms and coachmen, three housekeepers, and two men who spend all day winding up three hundred clocks…Someone who has an income of seven hundred and fifty thousand pounds, obtained rather dubiously, I'm afraid, from rack-rents, failing to repair, and kicking out the local Corns in favour of the more well heeled…How would Someone who buys their wife hundred thousand pound necklaces from Garrards; Someone who's been a party over the last twenty years to the shooting of a hundred and fifty thousand pheasants and the stalking of three thousand stags…

How would this Someone get the idea across to people that Small is Beautiful…?

…You see the difficulty?

And one's also trying to find ways of persuading people just to go back to being jolly nice.

But one's efforts only seem to lead to things like people being crushed to death, for example, whenever one simply walks about on visits.

One's mother gaily signs the Privy Council death warrants of hundreds of people from former Colonies, when there's no death penalty in this country, which is a bit off, though one doesn't want to say so.

One's grandmother has seventy-three servants, makes one squirm with embarrassment counting all the diamonds presented to her by De Beers on her trips to South Africa, appears to have had a rather cavalier attitude towards relations with learning difficulties, and thinks the Hilton Hotel is super if you look at it upside down.

One's aunt throws one's mother's dogs into the lake at Windsor in drunken fits of jealous spite.

The male members of one's family don't give one much support either. Edward has said he thinks caning is awfully good for children; Andrew delights in having six of the best from 'schoolgirls' in Hanky Spanky contests at Falklands Reunions; and one's father's letters to fading Hollywood starlets like Joan Caulfield have just been dug up, in which he raves on and on about her 'slappable bottom'.

> 'ONE'S NEVER QUITE SURE IF PEOPLE ARE AGREEING WITH ONE BECAUSE OF WHO ONE IS'

The upstairs and downstairs staff, and the crew of the Britannia, are ceaselessly involved in blue movie sessions and homosexual orgies, like maddened eunuchs.

Against this sultry background, and one's family showing one up, one's trying to get one's ideas across – things that one just thinks would be frightfully good for people to do.

…Do you see the problem?

And one has to be brief too, when one's trying to convey these brain-boggling notions. If one rabbits on for too long, one risks undermining the mystical power of the monarchy, which of course one believes in, and people might get the idea that one's human.

But, in a sense, that *is* what one's trying to drum into people's heads: human values and the human scale of things.

If one could sort of sum up what one's trying to do, it's to try and get the sixty-million-odd Estate workers in England, which I love, to realise that things would be much healthier if one's country was run more like a Jungian Gordonstoun, and people went back to being really simple.

And yet one only seems to be able to inspire people to send four human turds a week to Buckingham Palace; slash one's wife's portrait with lino-knives; produce pornographic souvenirs of very, very special events in one's life – on ash-trays, for Heaven's sake, so that people can sadistically stub their cigarettes out on oneself and one's spouse…to break into one's mother's bedroom to demand toys and clothes for their yobbish children in Hackney; to take pot-shots at one in a pathetic bid for momentary fame, and generally to regard one as a monstrous carbuncle.

One seems to have a neutering effect on anyone who gets close to one; or else people get so wound up at the thought of meeting one, that they get drunk and drive someone over after they leave.

It's all rather unbalanced.

All one seems to have achieved is the deforestation of an area the size of Outer Mongolia, so that newspapers can report every move one makes, every muscle one twitches.

Do you understand…?

Gosh, I'm so glad.

One's never quite sure if people are agreeing with one because of who one is.

POPE JOHN PAUL II

There's certainly more to the Pope (real name Pope John Paul II) than meets the eye. At least that's what we reckoned! So we sent along our super Starsleuth Fizz to find out. . .

He certainly wasn't disappontiffed (get it?) and we reckon neither will you.

In fact we reckon you'll be holy amazed!! (Ooh shut up Ed! – Fizz)

Favourite car: Popemobile.

Likes: Profiteroles, Sunbathing, Sending out Papal Bulls

Dislikes: When the Popemobile breaks down, Greasy hair, Missing exits on motorways, Tuna fish.

Relaxation: With a hectic life like mine, appearing to millions of people all over the world, it's really important to have a rest every now and then. On my nights off, I like to go to the cinema or occasionally a nightclub. Or sometimes I just stay at home and read *A Life of Christ* by Thomas à Kempis.

Favourite food: I'm a big fan of Chinese dishes and pretty handy with a wok! I really enjoy cooking for all my friends and most of them are still alive to tell the tale – honest!!

Favourite Papal Encyclical: I'm pretty pleased with *Dives in Misericordia*, but I suppose my real favourite's got to be *Redemptor Hominis*.

Pets: In my busy global schedule, I hardly have time to feed myself, let alone a load of pets. Although I wouldn't mind an Indian fruit bat.

Favourite Other High Ranking Prelate: Athenagoras, Ecumenical Patriarch of Constantinople.

Favourite Aftershave: Nina Ricci for Men. In a frantic job like mine, which involves meeting people and picking up babies all day long, it's essential to look good and above all to SMELL good!

Favourite Medieval Mystic: Dame Julian of Norwich.

Childhood heroes: My mum and dad.

What would you like to be if you weren't Pope?: Dalai Lama.

Favourite Poet: Pope.

Ambitions: Read the whole of the *Celestial Hierarchies* by St Dionysus the Areopagite without falling asleep.

Favourite T.V. Show: Brookside.

HIS HOLINESS THE POPE

JACK NICHOLSON

THE POSTMAN ALWAYS RINGS TWICE

(AND IF NO ONE ANSWERS HE JUST BASHES RIGHT THROUGH THE DOOR)

Jack Nicholson is perhaps the coolest man in the world. Let's face it – anyone who can make love to a young girl on a film set while her father looks on, has to have something. The Hustons did manage to save face to an extent by 'hiding' the scene in a feature film cunningly entitled *Prizzi's Honour*, whereas Nicholson's intention had been a 'short' to be dubbed *Jack's Oats*.

There is no denying the fact that Jack has it. It is difficult to find a chink in his armour. For instance, to criticise him for only having won 2 Oscars would seem, at best, churlish.

Let's face it. What do you say to the man who turned down the part of Butch Cassidy?

'Why did you turn down the part of Butch Cassidy?' would seem like a possible opener.

Many people believe Nicholson to be the Son of God. This belief was fuelled when Nicholson took the role of McMurphy in *One Flew Over the Cuckoo's Nest*. It later transpired, however, that the name McMurphy said backwards did not, in fact, sound like 'Jesus'.

Nicholson himself refutes the idea totally. As he put it, 'Well, perhaps I am. I don't know. I'm certainly related to God. I think he's my nephew.'

This obviously upset God – he hasn't spoken to him since. A fact which certainly hasn't bothered Jack.

In point of fact, it is Jack and not God who continues to land starring roles in major films, whereas his nephew – if indeed he is – has made infrequent appearances since his embarrassing and somewhat grandiose performance in the arrogantly titled *The Greatest Story Ever Told*.

CECIL PARKINSON

I have never liked Cecil Parkinson very much, so I was not looking forward to writing this piece. But the more deeply I researched him, the greater my respect and admiration became as I realised that we had more in common than I first thought.

I too have slimy hair.

I too give people the willies.

I too took a course of cheap elocution lessons which didn't work very well.

And I too had a mistress. Having one is *de rigeur* for virile, important, clammy men like me. But I've never admitted it to anyone before, and it is a tremendous relief to be able to come clean at last.

It's an even bigger relief, in some ways, that none of the contributions in this book are attributed to their author.

So, yes, I had a mistress. Yes, I too got her pregnant. And, yes, I dumped her too.

Off Beachy Head in a pair of concrete leg-warmers.

Yes, I murdered my mistress, and I don't care who knows it.

Oh God. Suddenly I find this confession is giving me an erection. Suddenly I crave a boxing match. Or a bus disaster. Or a pair of binoculars and a rented room across the street from a blind, embittered dentist in Salford. Anything which introduces the working classes to agonising pain.

But enough about me. Another person I'm rather similar to is Norman Tebbit. The following description of him (not written by me) may give you further clues as to my own identity. This is madness, *madness* — but I'm enjoying all this so much, I just can't help myself.

"Norman Tebbit emerged from Edmonton County Grammar School and a position in the Airline Pilots Union to become one of the new breed of down-market Tory politicians. He has a sardonic sense of humour (God couldn't possibly be a Socialist, he says, or He would have preserved the dinosaurs for reasons of compassion). I could have seen him as Mrs Thatcher's butler, sallow and not perfectly shaved, whispering sarcastic jokes behind a slightly soiled glove. In leather gear and having inherited his father's bike he appears as an ageing skinhead or one of politics more elderly Hell's Angels."

News of the World hacks please note the words 'soiled', 'leather', 'elderly', and 'behind'.

Oh God, oh God. The *risk*.

JOHN MORTIMER

MORTIMER, John Aloysius; *born* December 25th 1920. *Mother:* Mary. *Earthly father:* Joseph. *Educ.* St Middlebrow 1930–35, University of Soft Knocks, 1935–40. *Married* Penelope, books include: Another Dreary Sunday Lunch in Hampstead with Everyone Arguing and Carrying On (short stories) and The Axe Under the Throne: The Unknown Queen Mother (biography). Barrister, playwright, novelist and bon viveur. *Legal cases include:* Nothing Wrong with a Bit of Honest Filth (lost), No Reasonable Public School Educated Fellow Could Deny The Artistic Worth of Linda Lovelace (lost) and I'm Radical Enough to Admit to Enjoying Sex (lost). *Many TV and Radio appearances include:* Smug and Fat: A Portrait of the Artist (South Bank Show Special), Call My Bluff

(lost), Any Questions (lost) and Me and My Silly Voice (contribution to Start the Week, Radio 4). *TV and Radio Plays include:* Rumpole of the Bailey, More Rumpole of the Bailey, Just a Bit More Rumpole of the Bailey, Rumpole Turns Up Again, The Unstoppable Rumpole, Rumpole Rakes It In, Hello, It's Rumpole Again and many more including Platitudes Prescribed, A Voyage Around Myself (20 episodes) and Just One More Rumpole. *Books include:* Do you Believe in God and would you mind if I had a quick top-up? (collected interviews), Brideshead Revisited (with Evelyn Waugh) and the 40-volume Rumpole Collection. *Recreations:* Being chummy and a teensy bit controversial, eating. *Clubs:* Garrick, Wig and Pen. *Address:* The Vicarage, Much Conceit, Fatten Humble, Herts.

FERGIE & DI

Dearest Sarah and My dear Diana,

I have received the joint portrait for the 'See Fergie and Di Show' you propose to stage at Wembley Stadium. Unfortunately I have arranged a meeting there of the Additional Curates Society (of which I am Patron), so your show will not now take place.

This is the right moment, I feel, to congratulate you both on your respective images. Diana – you have created for the nation the ultimate impossible dream. As you know we chose you from a limited field. There are not so many personable virgins over the age of puberty that descend from the Stuart Kings – albeit illegitimately. I always liked your shy head-down approach and was only mildly alarmed by that deep-plunge black dress. Did someone really say: 'Wasn't that a mighty feast to set before a King?' You have made great inroads into fashion and you can now perform an important service for me. Norman Hartnell, very much the best in my view, are in a spot of bother. You will therefore wear their clothes exclusively for a year. May I say also that I do think you cope expertly at being married to the only man in London who is not in love with you.

Fergie, your image would seem to be that of the all-too possible dream. You have been described to me as the take me or leave me, but preferably take me girl. You have done the best job in effectively silencing my second son, whose erstwhile sobriquet of Randy Andy is fast becoming a forgotten myth. I was very taken with your performance in the Knock-Out show and have decided to ask you to succeed me as Patron of the Braemar Highland Festival.

On this point I am looking forward to having you both up in Scotland from 1st August until 8th October. It will be fun picnicking each day and should be a complete rest. In the evening we will all play charades together.

Finally, I am informed that you both gave your detectives the slip and visited a club called Stringfellows the other night. I recently confiscated Princess Michael's wig, so next time please may I come too?

I remain, ever yours affectionately.

Elizabeth R

P.S. Charles tells me the only rock he enjoys is Edinburgh rock.

COL. MU'AMMAR MUHAMMAD AL-GADDAFI

JUST DON'T CALL HIM LATE FOR THE JIHAD

Dear Madam Protocol,
My husband and I are hosting an intimate, top-secret dinner party that will be attended by Libyan strongman Colonel Mu'ammar al-Gaddafi. What are the proper forms of address I should use when greeting or introducing him?
— Perplexed of Pinner

Dear Perplexed,
Arabs are very touchy about titles, and Gaddafi is no exception. He prefers to be addressed by all his traditional honorifics, as well as some new ones he has thought up personally. On formal occasions, he is: By the mercy of Allah and the beard of the Prophet, Mu'ammar al-Gaddafi, Lion of Libya, Eagle of Islam, Riddle of the Sphinx, Sultan of Swat, Master of the Universe, Shores of Tripoli, Jewel of the Nile, Purple Rose of Cairo, Lord of the Jungle, Black Hole of Calcutta, Dog of Flanders, King of the Castle, Soup of the Day, Wings of Man, Wisdom of the East, Song of the South, Nanook of the North, Wicked Witch of the West, Knight of the Living Dead, Fruit of the Loom, Sheik of the Week, Hunk of the Month, Pet of the Year, Lord of the Flies, Leader of the Pack, Toast of the Town, King of the Road, Duke of Earl, Pick of the Litter, Mystery of the Old Mill, Most Likely to Succeed, Last of the Mohicans, Sale of the Century, House of the Rising Sun, Charles of the Ritz, Oil of Ulay, Wheel of Fortune, Cream of Wheat, Piece of the Rock, Red Badge of Courage, Great Balls of Fire, Lullaby of Broadway, Wrath of God.

Among intimates and family members, however, the haughty desert chieftain answers to such less elaborate titles as Keymaster, Great Poobah, Grand Illusion, Ghostbuster, and Mister Wonderful.

Three tips for a successful evening: Be sure all women present wear veils, do not serve pork, and count the silverware.

WOODY ALLEN & MIA FARROW

As Allen Konigsberg awoke one morning from uneasy dreams, he found himself transformed in his bed into an auteur.

Woody leaned back from the typewriter and smiled enigmatically. A nice opening paragraph. But was it, he wondered, an homage or plagiarism? And is there a difference? While shaving philosophically that very morning, he had given himself a nasty nick with Occam's razor, and was now having difficulty making such distinctions. For instance, had there been any real difference between Louise Lasser and Diane Keaton? Between Being and Nothingness? Lox and Nova? Was creating a body of cinematic works with the same plots and characters the same thing as repeating yourself?

Once again the sensitive pink tushie of his mind itched against the woollen underwear of the Big Questions. Was life worth living? Even paying retail? When Death came for him, could he convince the Grim Reaper to take Tony Roberts instead? If God is Just and Wise, how could *Platoon* have won?

Suddenly, several small grinning Oriental faces popped up from behind his typewriter. Had the communists invaded? he wondered. Or should he order Lo Mein?

'Mia! Would you for Chrissake get your kids outta here?'

Ms. Farrow shimmered wraithlike into the room, nibbling provocatively on a tulip. 'Scoot!' she squealed to her variegated brood, 'Or we'll send you all back where you came from!'

The whimsical Woodman flung an old Oscar at their vanishing forms and turned, more in sorrow than in anger, to his willowy intended.

'Di…I mean Lou…that is, Mia, darling. The engagement is off. I can't create in this domestic chaos. Imagine if Kafka, Camus, Kierkegaard, any of the big guys, had a wife and kids! They'd still be doing stand-up today!'

'We'll talk about it later, snookums,' replied the placid shiksa. 'Right now there's a photographer from *Life* waiting in the hall.'

'Oh yeah,' mused the Comic Genius. 'He's here to do a spread on how I avoid publicity. Do you know where my old unironed plaid shirt is, honey? And where are my glasses?'

'Honestly!' sighed Mia. 'Men!'

Woody looked around to see whom she was addressing.

KAFKA LEAGUE, KAFKA LEAGUE, KAFKA LEAGUE ONWARD,

—or—

He Never
Met a Morphosis
He Didn't Like

DR. DAVID OWEN & DAVID STEEL

Once upon an England he loved to waste a few foreigners with Martini-dry cracks from the cruelly arrogant mouth or the eager Berretta, in between finishing off *The Times* crossword and dressing for Ascot. The dinner-jacketed figure returning late to his bachelor flat, snapping on the indirect lighting for one stiff drink before casual puncturing of the quivering female inflatable in his bed: he showed every would-be swine in the world how to do it. Down in the basement amusing little men serviced the complicity of all males and groaned like dogs when – as was the masters' nature – they broke or scorned the gadgets of sadism.

But above all, he loved his little gun. Together they stood for breeding, sheer pedigree's easy command of mere technique and the hulking big battalions. Everything in their way got the same perfectly timed blast from reliable old snub-nose, who never failed to rise to the occasion.

Never... until the day after M collapsed at one of Cynthia's parties and a strangely uncoy Moneypenny snapped: 'Mrs No's taken over, and no-one keeps *her* waiting .'

'Well, Dr Yes,' the saw-faced lady inside sneered from under an obvious blonde wig, 'we're cutting back. A Ford for you instead of that Aston Martin, and from now on every cartridge is accountable to Q here.'

Behind her Q smirked quietly: the suburbanite's day had come at last. 007 swallowed hard: 'I'm all for reform,' he gasped, 'but this is against tradition, it'll never work.'

'Get busy,' hissed Mrs No, bracketing him with blue eyes far steelier than his own. 'I will accept no excuses.'

007 felt the Force begin to drain out of him: the only way out was to shoot this woman, immediately. He reached for the comforting shape and up it came. But to his horror it wouldn't fire. Then, suddenly with a mind of its own, it wriggled violently in his grasp and pointed straight between his own eyes. 'I've always wanted to do this, you bastard,' it squeaked, just before the last detonation. Everything went blue, forever.

The dinner-jacketed figure returned late to his bachelor flat, snapping on the indirect lighting for one stiff drink before casual puncturing of the quivering female inflatable in his bed ...

LETHAL ALLIANCE

ANDREW LLOYD WEBBER

WHO'S WHO

LLOYD WEBBER, Andrew Amadeus Bach; *born* Sterling February 14th 1949. *Educ.* London School of Economics, Institute of Chartered Accountants, Val Doonican Institute of Further Music. *Married* Gillian Perfectly-Nice (1969). *2nd m.* Sarah Maria Callas Brightman. Composer and impresario. *Operas include:* Tim-rice and His Amazingly Paltry Lyrics, Jesus Christ Superstar!, Evita!, Cats! (with T.S. Eliot), Skates!, Puppies!, Song and Dance!, One Sings, The Other Sues, and Requiem for Being Taken Seriously. *Hit songs include:* 'Jesus Christ, La La La', 'Evita, La La La', 'Don't Cry for Me, Bankamanaga', 'The Same Song in Another Show', 'Cats, La La La' and many others including I can't remember offhand but he must have done others, he *must* have done. *Owner of many theatres including:* All in Great Britain except The Theatre Upstairs, Stockport and The Palladium, Bromley (co-owner) and, as impresario, widely credited with the great revival of musicals by Andrew Lloyd Webber between 1977 and 1987. *Numerous television appearances include:* But That Sounds Like Someone Else's: The Music of Andrew Lloyd Webber (LWT) and The Immortal Tunes of Andrew Lloyd Webber (6 mins). *Future projects include:* Don Giovanni! (with W.A. Mozart) and Bragg!, a rock-opera based on the life and times of Melvyn Bragg. *Recreations:* Not having any rows at all with Sarah Brightman, suing anyone who claims he has, looking rat-faced, placing exclamation marks at the end of new musicals. *Address:* The Banks, Much-of-a-Muchness, Berks.

> 'IT'S REALLY ABOUT A MAN WHO IS HIDEOUSLY UGLY FROM BIRTH, BUT A GENIUS, AND WHO FALLS HOPELESSLY IN LOVE WITH THIS GIRL AND IS ONLY ABLE TO EXPRESS HIMSELF THROUGH MUSIC'

Andrew Lloyd Webber on *The Phantom of the Opera, Sunday Express Magazine,* 28.9.86.

SYLVESTER STALLONE

YEAR DATE ≫

5 MILLION PLUS ONE.
REPORT ON EARTH MISSION
FOR LIFESPURT.

LOCATE ≫

ANCIENT CITY OF LOS
ANGELES

STRANGE BEING FOUND
SUSPENDED IN ICE POD. ON
TIME HOLD FOR RESUSS.

Man length > 5ft 6in {earth code} Enhanced by shoe hydraulic. Logo reads > *'LIFTS BY MAN-STRETCHER—S. BOULEVARD.'*

Creature suffering muscle fake well in excess of frame build. But oversize not evidenced in rudiment repro area — Seed Tube not in scale. Possible reason for race extinction?

Examination of face hole area reveals packed white biters. China repro crown ins. Plus tongue unit *minus* usual muscle factor. Not compatible with human speech mode. Lip sur-round locked in sneer signal. Possible subject communicated by Grunt Factor. Eyes suffer lid droop—subject only capable of 'Slitvision'.

Usual Humanoid skin cover but tint up with tribal brown pigment with oily gloss slime applicate. Artifactos found near man, point ups maybe?
Logos read > *'MANTANFASTIC'* plus *'K—Y Gel.'*

Primary Brain Scan shows muscle develop in head box. Even when alive likely that, in Human-speak, man was 'Braindead'. Man clutches small totem Logoread > *'Presented By The Academy For Lifetime Achievement.'* History data reveals—totems given to peoples known as 'actors'. People paid to pretend to be other peoples.

ERGO FACTOR ≫ 'Gruntman' is prime example of Century 20 actor stroke peoples.

CONCLUSION ≫ Human Race—Century 20. Peopled by Pygmy Man on Stiltlift plus Slitvision. Oiled and dyed skin cover. All muscle fake — save Seedtube. Minus grey brain bits and expected speech modes. Resuss possible with mod tech but Culture ops advise against. Man supposed too primitive for adaptation to 'Now' period.

RECOMMEND ≫ WASTE HIM.

JAMES ANDERTON

CBE, QPM, CHIEF CONSTABLE, GREATER MANCHESTER POLICE FORCE

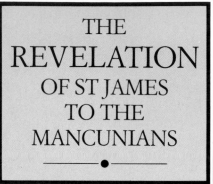

THE
REVELATION
OF ST JAMES
TO THE
MANCUNIANS

1 And he came before them saying, I was proceeding through the centre of Manchester about my lawful occasions when, lo, the heavens were rent asunder and a flashing blue light shone round about.

2 And a voice spake unto me saying, James, James.

3 And I was sore afraid, in spite of my many years' experience in dealing with aliens, cranks and outright revolutionary nutters.

4 And the voice spake again saying, James, I haven't got all day.

5 And I cried out with a loud voice saying, Lord, Lord, I'm all ears. Well, all ears and truncheon.

6 For I did recognise the voice from a previous meeting on the golf course at Wythenshawe.

7 And the Lord said unto me, Look James, the thing is this. Man gurgleth about in a cesspool of his own devising and since thou, James, art my servant in whom I have made a considerable investment in real terms, I look unto thee for suggestions.

8 And I was filled with an exceeding joy and cried out saying, Lord, say no more, for I will throw the Book at them.

9 And the countenance of the Lord shone forth from a beacon, as it was written in the book of the prophet Belisha, and the Lord did wink with an exceeding great wink, and saith unto me, whither thou patrollest I shall patrol, and even as thou scratchest my back, so shall I scratch thine also.

10 And I lifted up mine eyes and said unto Him, Lord, thou art a white man. By the way, I like the beard.

11 Thus spake James to the people.

12 And the people answered not straightway, but went their way grumbling and saying, stone us, we have heard of the Flying Squad.

13 But this is ridiculous.

SIR LAURENCE OLIVIER & SIR JOHN GIELGUD

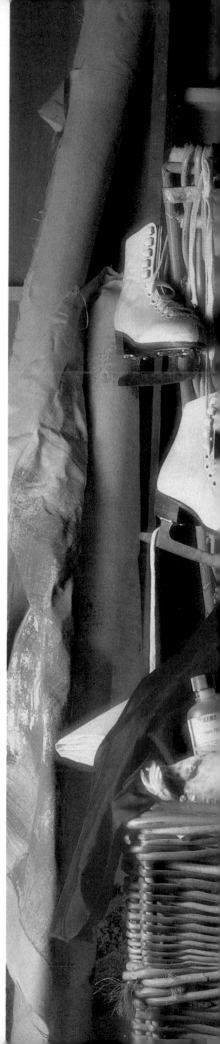

OLIVIER made his début at the age of ten as Brutus in Julius Caesar. His staggeringly mature performance was somewhat overlooked in the furore that surrounded his size. As the *Cleethorpes Times* put it 'We are asked to believe that Brutus was no more than three feet two inches tall. This is surely nonsense! I cannot accept the conceit (dramatic or otherwise) that Brutus required a pair of kitchen stepladders in order to stab Caesar.' The *Dartington Herald* was less kind, the entire review running to no more than three words – 'Et tu, Shorty.'

Devastated, Olivier refused to return to the stage until he was at least 5ft 9in. Ten years later, at the height of 5ft 8¾in., Olivier took a chance and appeared in the musical revue *Pass the Punt, Dickie.* This time the critics were unanimous in their praise. 'Laurence Olivier really is quite tall!' screamed the *Telegraph. The Times* went further, 'With raised heels and a straw boater, Olivier could pass for six feet plus.'

His confidence boosted, over the next thirty years Olivier was to give some of his tallest performances. These include Hamlet (5ft 10½in.), Richard III (with calipers, 6ft 1in.), and Shallow in Henry IV (with that big floppy hat, an incredible 6ft 6in.). His stage career culminated in his portrayal of Akash in the musical *Time* where his head alone measured 40ft from ear to ear. Lord Olivier is now an incredibly old man who thinks he's a telephone.

GIELGUD'S début was as Hamlet, portraying him as a tall English gentleman. This triumph was followed by his Antony, who he interpreted as a tall English gentleman. Henry VIII was scaled down to suit Gielgud's very personalised view of this famous king: Gielgud suggested that perhaps he was really quite thin, quite tall and quite posh. Macbeth, Shylock and Othello followed, played as thin, tall and posh respectively.

Considering his reputation for playing tall English gentlemen, many believed the real Gielgud to be other than a tall English gentleman. Some thought he might be a squat Welshman for example, and were surprised to discover that he was, in fact, a tall English gentleman. (Interestingly enough, Gielgud did once play a squat Welshman, but he played him as a tall English gentleman.)

But Gielgud was propelled onto the world stage when, in 1965, he heard the word 'fuck' for the first time. The seed of an idea was planted, and when 5 years later Gielgud heard it again he realised the limitless possibilities of a tall English gentleman who said 'fuck'. He has gone on to say 'fuck' in 13 major motion pictures.

(N.B. In the Olivier v. Gielgud debate, it is almost impossible to say who is the greater, although what is certain is that they're both better than that bloke who plays Ken Barlow.)

> **The above is an extract from Terence Hack's *From Titch to Bighead: Licking up to Larry* (£9.95).**

Back in the Sixties, on Newcastle Town Moor, where every Summer a great two-week fair was held, one of the more dramatic sideshows featured *Misty, Psychic.* A lustrous oiled teendream in sequined bra and sateen harem pantaloons, like some Geordie Little Egypt, she sported a winking glass eye in her navel, multicoloured veils trimmed out of discarded tights and, for her living, she ate hit records.

Blindfolded, she would be fed a random diet of unplayed 45s, which she proceeded to chomp upon like vinyl ginger snaps, swallow wholesale. After allowing herself a moment to inwardly digest, she would then name both singer and song.

She rarely if ever failed. No sound in creation was so arcane, no production so dense that she could not capture them. For every timbre, rhythm, riff, it seemed, there was an answering echo. But her very favourites were Ben E. King and the Drifters. At first munch she knew them, *Under The Boardwalk, Up On The Roof,* and contentedly she burped. Elvis, by contrast, she would ingest with piety like a First Communion wafer; whereas a Bob Dylan or Val Doonican she endured with wrinkled nose, as if they were cod-liver oil. But all of them went down, regardless; and stayed down, too.

All, that is, until Tina Turner. Just one mouthful of *River Deep, Mountain High,* however, then Misty gagged, gave out a sawn-off screech, and back in a flood came the whole mess of potage, like molten lava, too hot and too fierce to control. 'No power alive,' Misty mumbled, when breath and reason returned, 'could keep *that* woman down.'

YES, BUT CAN SHE COOK...?

NEIL KINNOCK

Once upon a time there was a little fellow called Kinnochio who had a big heart, came with no strings attached and, although sometimes slightly wooden, always tried to tell the truth.

He had some lovely ideas too, about free health and education, banning bombs, Union rights, not being horrid to gay people. Just the sort of thing to make him lots of nice friends, and of course it did.

Unfortunately Kinnochio had a problem. There was a gang of terrible bullies who used to shout at him and flick the V's and deliberately distort all his nice ideas. They said that if you made friends with Kinnochio a huge slavering Cossack would fly in on an SS20 and force your children to become Lesbians. They said Kinnochio had a terrible disease called the 'Loony Trots' and you'd catch it if you got too close.

They said these horrid things because they wanted to keep all their power and cash for themselves and they

knew Kinnochio wanted to spread it about a bit. But they wouldn't talk about that, they just kept taunting him, and making his life a misery, often using their ultimate insult, calling him *left wing*.

Kinnochio was left wing, and he was proud of it, but instead of standing up and saying 'There's nothing loony about all my nice ideas you just want to hang on to your cash' he began to lie a bit. He began to try to make the bullies like him, by pretending that he didn't believe in things quite so much as he actually did. So the more people called Kinnochio left wing, the more he tried to

pretend he wasn't. And all the gay people, and black people, and people who didn't want to get fried in a nuke war, and miners who had fought to keep the pits open, began to wonder whether he was left wing at all, but in fact a closet Tory like Wilsonio or Callaghanio.

When the *Pinnochio* lied, his nose got longer.

When Labour politicians forget their principles, you get the Winter of Discontent. Only time will tell how Little Kinnochio turns out. Here, Glenys is reminding him of Jiminy Cricket's immortal line 'Always let your conscience be your guide.'

HER MAJESTY THE QUEEN

(Elizabeth Schleswig-Holstein-Sonderberg-Glückstein-Battenburg, a.k.a. Guelph, now known as Windsor-Mountbatten)

The Christmas Broadcast…

Yes, I'm thinking about it now,

very deeply. Do go away.

' …Good afternoon, objects.

How wonderful to see you grovelling yet again for another piece of green paper with my face upon it – of which a large proportion reverts to me through the good auspices of my Government. When We first came to the throne in 1953, a pound was worth a pound. Now it is worth twenty-six pence. We are extremely grateful to you all for the missing seventy-four pee.

We have tried to keep abreast of the times: the Queen's Bounty of £3.00 for triplets, established in 1849, has been discontinued. We also now have only two birthdays: one official, and one unofficial; as opposed to the former three: one official, one unofficial, and one real.

It may not have escaped your attention that the Royal Family is England's only surviving industry, and we have consequently put on a Royal Event of international significance every summer for the last thirty years to attract visitors from foreign parts.

An event chosen recently for this purpose was my son's wedding. He was married to a young slip of a girl, Diana Spencer; the step-grand-daughter of the distinguished novelist Barbara Cartland, a woman who has done almost as much for the English language as we have done for the human spirit.

Diana Windsor is a girl beyond criticism, a girl who, at nineteen years of age, realised the dream of every woman in the country: a fairy-tale romance, marriage, and early motherhood. A girl with whom we are more than happy to share our limelight and shotguns.

I see my mission in life to believe what my advisers instruct me to believe. I have a large house at the end of the Mall with six hundred and fourteen rooms. I visit many of them and think therein of my duties towards you all. Towards the homeless, the poor and the ill at ease.

And, if my thoughts do not bear fruit there, then Balmoral, Sandringham, Windsor, Holyrood House, Kensington Palace, Hampton Court, Birkhall and Royal Lodge, Clarence House, Fort Belvedere, and the Castle of Mey, Chevening, St James's Palace, and Gatcombe Park … great think-tanks strategically placed up and down our country… are available to me.

We live in a democracy as you know, so, do drop me a line about anything you feel we might be able to help you with.

And let us now, this Christmas, remember the words of Campbell Bannerman, a famous Royal Gillie: "Hypocrisy is sexy," and let us all prepare to tighten our belts together to the sound of this inspired and enriching hymn … GOD SAVE THE QUEEN '

> It has been calculated that the interest upon my wealth would give every man, woman and child in this country an income of £15.00 a week. You may say that this is not to be sniffed at; but, with inflation as it is, I'm sure that you'll agree it is a negligible amount, a mere drop in the ocean. Our family has been used to wealth, and, in the words of a famous theologian: 'Only the posh deserve to rule.'

MIKHAIL GORBACHEV

MIKHAIL GORBACHEV woke with a start. He had it. He had the idea. He knew how to stop the whole arms race at a stroke. It was controversial, but it was brilliant. He suddenly saw that it was all a question of symbols and mistrust, and the way to defeat the mistrust was through the symbols. First, he would withdraw his troops from Afghanistan. Next, he would take his advisors out of everywhere in South America. Finally, he would accede to the destruction of the Berlin Wall, while of course, keeping a full guard there. All three things would not fundamentally affect Russia's welfare, but they were of such profound symbolic importance to the Americans that they would have to drop SDI immediately, and start the process of complete disarmament.

He juggled in his mind who to ring first – the Chief of Staff, the East German president, or Fidel Castro. Undecided for a moment, he lay back in bed.

'Awake so early?', muttered Raisa, and snuggled up towards him. He always loved her in the morning, soft & warm, with the remains of last night's mascara speckled down her cheek.

'Yes – I've had a wonderful idea – it will change the world,' replied Mikhail.

'O, who's a clever boy,' she said, and leaned over further to kiss him. He didn't move, but his lips were soft and receptive, not hard as they were when he was unhappy. She kissed him again, and this time, their lips both parted.

It was that moment when you know. Slowly, she slipped off her slight white nightdress and unbuttoned his grey pyjamas. Mikhail turned gently and took her in his arms. How lovely she is, he thought, as beautiful to me as the first time I glimpsed her sitting next to Koleshnikov at the KGB Annual Dinner Dance.

But soon they were past thought – making love as they always had, love full of passion and drive, but coated with a gentleness made of true affection. Body locked into body and the duvet slipped away as they came together with a double cry of satisfaction.

For a moment there was silence, then she dropped gently back onto the sheets.

'You were saying, my little darling – you had an idea.'

'Did I?'

He searched his memory, but all he could remember was the gentle curve of her thigh, and the soft pit of her stomach.

'Nope. All gone. Pass me the phone will you – I promised to talk to the Chief of Staff first thing about this new laser breakthrough – at last we've got those damn Yanks where we want them. Roll on world domination!!!'

Then kissing her one final time, he headed off to the bathroom to paint on his scar and thought to himself – 'What kind of world would it be without love?'

MARGARET THATCHER, PM

LEADERSHIP

Of the many very bizarre yarns on the theme of Leadership to be found in the Old Testament, none is stranger than that concerning the so-called Golden Cow. The Israelites, a go-getting, consumer-orientated society, were growing increasingly cheesed off with the then Prime Minister, Moses, a whiskery old cove of pious demeanour with a line in somewhat outré conjuring tricks.

His crass mismanagement of the economy had led to a long period of austerity, obliging the Superpower of the day to airlift in emergency supplies of what was called 'Manna': now that the GNP had taken something of an upturn, the old boy condemned the electorate's natural desire to better themselves from a material point of view as 'idolatry', or 'whoring after Strange Gods'.

Not being a leader of any real calibre, he was forced to bring in the aforementioned Superpower to threaten sanctions. Even though his neighbours in Egypt had strongly resented this; the Gippos drawing the line at being bombarded with frogs, hailstones and boils on the bum, which they saw as unwarranted interference in their internal affairs.

As Brother Moses, however, was hot-footing it down from a summit conference with the Superpower, confident of a general acceptance of his so-called Ten Commandments, he espied the Party Faithful having a knees-up in his absence, adoring a Golden Cow.

Margaret Hilda Thatcher has proved herself a Leader of infinitely greater stature: if the troops don't fancy some grisly hike up the moral uplands, get the market analysts to find out where they do want to go and tell them to 'come on down'. She is seen here adoring a Sacred Golden Cow, Winnie T.

Dear Ernest Eggnogge,

I've received some whining, snivelling, wipe my eyes, pass the Kleenex, letters in my time, but yours truly takes the Huntley and Palmers. Quite frankly I don't give a toss that your old mother died of hypothermia last winter or that your zit-faced moronic teenaged lout of a son has not worked since leaving school. And the news that your wife has been waiting for six years to have her nasty infected womb removed left me cold. Haven't you got a sharp knife for God's sake?

You dare to say that I am 'out of touch with real people' and suggest I 'jump on a train and come up North'.

Firstly, Mr. Eggnogge, I am married to a 'real person'. Secondly, I would rather spend the night with Guy the Gorilla (Yes, I know he's dead) than climb aboard one of those vile rattling contraptions and visit you all up there in slag heap land. We have nothing in common. I hate ferrets, dripping, pigeons, corner shops and fat, ugly, pale people who are unable to speak in complete sentences and who don't understand how the International Monetary Fund works.

Finally, at the end of your letter you bleat on about your dole payment calling it 'a pittance' and an 'affront to your dignity'. This last bit made me laugh quite a lot. What did you get for Christmas? A subscription to *New Society*?

Listen parasite, that's the point, don't you see? We don't need you and your sort anymore – get the message now? Take my advice, shovel the coal out of the bath, then fill it up and jump in and drown yourself.

N.B. Note to Private Secretary: Tidy this up a bit will you?

10 DOWNING STREET,
WHITEHALL, S.W.1.

Dear Mr Eggnogge,

The Prime Minister was most concerned to hear of your difficulties. She is looking into the various matters you raised in your letter.

Yours sincerely,

Rupert Brown-Bear

BOB HOSKINS AND MICHAEL CAINE

Mickey and Bob, beneath a Hockney-blue sky, beside a Hockney-blue pool, full of fat conger eels. They sing:

Maybe it's because I'm a Londoner
That I love jellied eels
Maybe it's because I'm a Londoner
That I shop at Gimpel Fils
I get a funny feeling inside of me
Just walking through Bel Air
Maybe it's because I'm a Londoner
That I'm hardly ever there.

Maybe it's because I'm a Londoner
That I support West Ham
Maybe it's because I'm a Londoner
That I ask Albert Roux for Spam
I get a funny feeling inside of me
Just walking round my Merc
Maybe it's because I'm a Londoner
That I'm a total berk.

Maybe it's because I'm a Londoner
That I get patronised
Maybe it's because I'm a Londoner
That I win the Oscar prize
I get a funny feeling inside of me
Just walking to the bank
Maybe it's because I'm a Londoner
My last five movies stank.

Maybe it's because I'm a Londoner
That I'm the king of Cannes
Maybe it's because I'm a Londoner
I make Sean Penn look like
               Renaissance Man
I get a funny feeling inside of me
Just walking through Monterey
Maybe it's because I'm a Londoner
That I've moved to L.A.

Bob, Mike's bosom buddy, hails from Brisbane. He played bass with Frank Ifield for eleven years before getting national recognition in T.V.'s *Auf Wiedersehen Barnet*. He has got very flustered in some of his best work, and was recently nominated for getting perturbed and vexed in *John Garfield goes to Sainsbury's*. When asked his favourite colour, he said what of?

Glaswegian Mike, a leggy blonde, modelled bear-brand stockings before being discovered in his late forties in the early sixties. His work with Cilla Black got him very big, and his girth spread far as the espionage cook in Paul Simon's *Zulu*. His sojourn in L.A. culminated in his recent return to these shores, and nowadays he does cheesecake for Langan bras and goes out for ninepence in sunny climes. There are doubts about the mantle of Bogarde being draped around these hungry shoulders, but old Mike's had a jolly good crack for all that.

Well hullooo . . . and a very good DAY; though I'm afraid the outlook is really very MISERABLE – beginning as we do with some really very DAMP showers of excuses for JOKES at the expense of foreign, ah, goalkeepers, falling among an impenetrable MIST of sitcom previews in the, ah, CAMDEN area . . . followed all too quickly by a really very serious outbreak of LEPRECHAUNS in our theme parks; clearly, a six-figure salary is simply, ah, IN-ADEQUATE. But now, just WATCH here – as my hands circle like AIRPLANE PROPELLORS at the prospect of the leprechaun storm bringing with it these really very DENSE clouds of FEAR, obscuring Pamela Stephenson from VIEW for all TIME . . . or at least until these really very soft and lisping CASCADES of DUMPLINGS and DEARIES fall cosily upon us from a

PRINCE

LITTLE MAN, YOU'VE HAD A BUSY DAY.

IAN BOTHAM

Brisbane,
Australia

The England Touring Team
World Cup
Pakistan

G'day, you stupid bunch of Pommie bastards!

Look how quick I've copped the strine! I'm right in it.

Strewth, these Queensland banana—benders are a bunch of bonzer folk. You don't need a ghost writer to talk to them, no worries.

The Big Smell, Sir Joh Bjelke—Petersen, is so far right he's off the continental shelf and into the bloody Pacific. His wife Flo has just stopped us switching to summer—time. Reckons it fades the curtains. Straight up, these are people I can relate to.

Yeah, this is really my kind of country. Plenty of sun, sand, sea, surf, stubbles, steak, and they think foreplay is something you do in the nets. My old mate Thommo reckons I'd make a good Aussie. He's out here as you probably know. Seems to have lost the plot a bit — given up cricket and started growing flowers, for Christ's sake!

Not that it's easy being a legend these days, and don't I know it. The old chassis isn't what it was, and the bowling's not the only thing that's gone to pot. There's still a lot of huffing and puffing, spitting and snorting, mind you. But it's mostly just to get the jock—strap on.

I sometimes think the memory's a few bangers short of a barbie, as well. You'll laugh, but I even miss reading all that crap about me in the Pom tabloids. And writing for them, too. Then I think, for forty grand a year, why worry? Out here, I don't get out of bed for that sort of money.

But don't get me wrong. There's still a lot of pressure to perform. Duncan Fearnley and the car phone boys don't just shell out top dollar for a foaming drongo. I know Dill gets away with it, but he's only fit every other Wednesday when there's an 'r' in the month, and I've got a reputation to keep up.

I spend a bit of time writing too, as you can see — doing a touch of the John Snow's, if you want the truth. They like a good limerick out here, so I thought I'd do a whole book of them for Collins. Here's one:

There was once this terrific, amazingly tall,
   dark(ish), handsome, brilliant and tal-
   ented all—rounder (me),
Who couldn't believe that the Somerset
   dressing room thought he was a complete
   tosspot, and got rid of him, and so he
   threatened to have Peter Roebuck puréed in
   the magimix, er, for tea.
'But I'm a living legend,' he said,
'So I'm off to Brizzie instead.
'Because you lot are about as much fun as a
   dingo at the Nativity!'

Put it on the dunny wall, Gatt. You can read it when you're next in the runs.

G'night.

Both

Both

RONALD & NANCY REAGAN

Dear Lawfluck,

For that I am of yr. tasteful inventions, you so too far when you suggest that an actor like Ronald Reagan could ever be president of what Spiro Agnew, with characteristic verve and originality, hailed as "the greatest nation in the country". — I fear that I must pass, lover of the bizarre that I am —

[signature]

Dear Lawfluck

Fan that I am of yr tasteful inventions, you go too far when you suggest that an actor like Ronald Reagan could ever be president of what Spiro Agnew, with characteristic verve and originality, hailed as "the greatest nation in the country" – I fear that I must pass, lover of the bizarre that I am.

MICHAEL JACKSON

CREATURE THE EARTH FORGOT

Three White men, Jews in the money trade, came out of the East and journeyed to Los Angeles, there to meet with Michael Jackson and negotiate themselves a piece of the Jacksons' forthcoming tour, which was entitled *Victory.* Three Black men, Muslims in the money trade, intercepted them at LAX Airport, and all six together drove to a Jackson mansion in the Valley.

It was mid-morning when they arrived but no host greeted them. Michael had only recently emerged from hospital, surfacing from his latest martyrdom by plastic surgery. Previously his nose and lips and hair, the cleft of his chin, his teeth and his eyebrows had all been born again. This time his cheekbones and the shaping of his eyes had also been recast. He was now entirely his own second coming.

Somewhere inside a sterilised room far upstairs, like the boy in the bubble, he hid cocooned in an oxygen tent, with only one mirror for company. Meantime, the three Black and three White men must practise patience, all dressed up in hungers, no Thriller to ease the ache.

The entire day they waited, slicing and reslicing the ET overhead into ever minuter slivers, and as tempers frayed, so did racial harmony. Twilight brought breaking point. Then suddenly the dealers were aware that they no longer wheeled alone.

A shadow stood watching from the doorway. In silence it approached. And as it entered the pool of green gamblers' light that bathed their table, and they could see it plain, the men recognised it at once: here was the Invisible Man.

Not a scrap of its flesh lay exposed. The white bandages that swaddled every feature were echoed by the silken scarf that masked the throat, the skintight doeskin glove on the right hand, a dazzlement of teeth so pearly they might have been pawned off Diana Ross; the eyes were locked beyond impenetrable wraparound shades; the other hand lurked inside the pocket of a white male nurse's robe; and even the hair, denatured by unkinking and endless waving, seemed sprayed on, *a piece,* not even its kiss-curl for real.

As this mirage shimmered before them, the money men quailed, petrified in case it be sickened by their squabblings and drive them from the temple. So, in a panic to cover up, one voice began to blather, thrash about at random. 'All we were saying,' it blurted, 'This tour is a tour that knows no barriers, it's for the people, all the people, everywhere, regardless of colour, creed or chemicals of choice. I mean, it's for folks. For just plain folks.'

Michael Jackson made no answer. For long moments he stayed still, he pondered. Then he drew out his left hand from its pocket and laid it in the green light, palm upwards. Its skin looked brand new, the softest roseate pink, like a baby's; the high-pitched whisper came so faint, so expressionless, the men could barely catch it: 'The last time I looked,' intoned the Invisible Man, 'I believe I was still Black.'

RUPERT MURDOCH

Hello Possums

Goodness only knows what kind of pickie the publishers intend teaming with this little composition of mine. Knowing those irreverent, zany, whacky, no-holds-barred Spitting Image scallywags, I bet their puppet of my old chum Rupert Murdoch is no oil painting (yet I have known spooky instances where the SI mask was *more attractive* than the real thing though John Mortimer and Andrew Lloyd Webber probably wouldn't agree).

My guess is the Editor of this publication wants me to 'tip the bucket' on the famous Australian publisher, to use an old Aboriginal expression whose origins have been lost in the mists of time. But how could I do that?

Rupe is an old Melbourne pal of mine from way back; I first learnt to read about the Big Wide World in one of his father's wonderful newspapers. Let's face it possums, if I was such a foolish old megastar as to bad-mouth our eminent Australian impresario, I would do two terrible things: wreck our long and warm friendship and run the risk of affectionate annihilation from the Murdoch press next time I do one of my wonderful shows. Wouldn't I be silly to stick my gem-encrusted neck out? In my book Rupert Murdoch is a *Saint* in a sad old country (the UK) where guts and enterprise are still dirty words, I'm sorry but they are.

(Dictated by the Authoress, on her in-car fax machine en route to a celebrity lunch at the News of the World)

THE TIMES
MEMORANDUM

From: Rupert Murdoch | To: Charlie Wilson

Date: 20.7.87

Charlie Wilson, Editor of The Times, with a frank appraisal of Rupert Murdoch.

Once a lustrum there bursts, with all the triumphal splendour of an Hadrian or an Trajan, into the forum of international affairs an figure so gigantic, so profoundly radical, so endowed with an vivid sense of justice, freedom, honesty, freedom and above all, freedom, that it is hard to beat down an erection when thinking about him. Margaret Thatcher was one such, and in our opinion so too was Ted Rogers. But if one supremely shining figure is to stand out in our age as an genuine hero it is hard to think of one more uniquely qualified than Rupert Murdoch.

With courage, determination and selfless sacrifice he has carved out an Empire of freedom and choice in the once bloodied battleground of union tyranny and pisshearted liberal wingeing. An Empire that stretches across the globe, an Empire on which the Sun is never type-set.

Uniquely placed not just to sell newspapers and television programmes, Murdoch is able to sell ideas: ideas that in their scope, breadth, ambit and sheer fucking ball-breaking spunkiness, will make sure that no half-arsed acorn-cocked turd-burglar is ever going to find an outlet for the kind of vomit-flecked commie crap propaganda those shit bags in the BBC spew out every bleeding day. I wouldn't piss up their arses if their kidneys were on fire.

Freedom of speech and moral cleanliness are the texts of this awesome latter day Savonarola. This newspaper, his flagship, and its proud sister vessels The Sun and The News of the World stand proud testament to his staggering achievement in taking Britain down the road to quality, choice, independence, freedom and breasts.

There you go charlie, shove in a few long words for chrissake and put in something about the BBC. My Sky channel is still getting pissawful ratings.

Love Roops

MERYL STREEP, ROBERT DE NIRO AND DUSTIN HOFFMAN

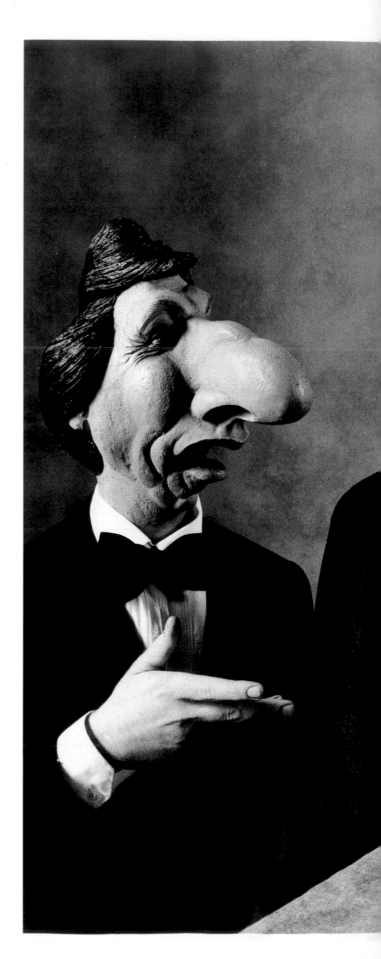

The highest symbol of spiritual and mental development is the movie star. (The 'B' and 'C' actors, not so much.) Once we were tiny fishes, millennia ago. It was thanks to a Being greater than ourselves from another planet, and our own remarkable wisdom, that we were able to return to Earth and command five million dollars a picture, thus aiding and assisting the souls of lesser incarnates.

Ours is a difficult path on which to travel. Some of us have been making fools of ourselves, by revealing information not privy to your average filmgoer. Our information is secret, and revealed here *now* for the first time.

Outwardly, we are highly gracious and modest; for despite our brilliance, and our remarkable ability to portray a myriad, infinite variety of characters – yes, characters in depth, including REMARKABLE accents, appearance, psyche and even multiple sexes – the true essence of our present incarnation continues to shine through, hence the public's ability to recognise us always as 'Meryl', 'Dustin' and 'Robert' as earlier peons knew us as Descartes, Caesar and Elvis.

It is hard to have reached the pinnacle of such spiritual evolution; harder still to be the conduit of such infinite wisdom. From an early age we received Love and Abeyance – our mothers in particular recognised us for who we were on first sight – and our path has been a long and difficult one, but we are not complaining, no, for the *path to true greatness* is fraught with the Stanislavsky method and the Yale School of Drama, and also working as a waiter, though of course none of us had to do that except for maybe a couple of weeks during the summer, so readily was our great and extraordinary genius recognised.

Making a movie isn't easy, of course, nobody really understands how TRULY TRULY difficult it is, to assume a character, to *become* that character and sit around for hours and weeks on some movie lot and just sit there for hours and hours while make-up is applied and the brilliance is simply pouring forth and the five million dollar cheque collects interest, for money of course means NOTHING to us, not a goddamn thing, for we are BEYOND MONEY and are ONE WITH ART.

For the *first time ever* we are able to make our knowledge available; while others, too insignificant to mention here, blew our cover before they were supposed to, we have now received information that *for a limited time only* a select few may obtain the SECRET WISDOM OF THE STARS.

You may think this is unbelievable. Yet every statement that has just been stated is documented and certified true. For a limited time only, 100% MONEY BACK GUARANTEE, *THE WISDOM OF THE MYSTIC MOVIESTARS* is the POWER to BE in CONTROL. ORDER NOW, send only $29.95 to Meryl, Robert and Dustin.

EDWINA CURRIE

'Hello there, Mrs Devine. It is Mrs Devine, isn't it? Do you know who I am? My goodness, do they call me that? Ha ha. It's better than Flabby Tits, isn't it? I think it's rather a compliment myself.

Now then Mrs Devine. I have popped in for a little chat with you. Why you? It's about this open heart surgery you are wanting. Triple by-pass? My word. Fabulous, isn't it, what the doctors can do these days? Mrs D., do you know how much an operation like that costs at today's prices? Well, I think you ought to give a shit. Before your government invests all that money in you, we want to be sure that you're genuinely seeking health. That's fair, isn't it? No, Mrs D., freedom from pain is *not* the same thing.

Look at you, lying there like a beached whale. You don't need me to tell you that you are grossly overweight. Nobody could call *you* Iron Tits, could they, Mrs D.? Ha ha. Mrs Devine, there were no fatties in Belsen. No, I wasn't there, Mrs Devine. You are fat because you eat too much. Too much rubbish. A thousand egg-and-chips and I'd look like you. You smoke. No, your daughter-in-law didn't tell me. I can tell by looking at you. You're kippered. Your breath smells like rusty nails.

Do you know, Mrs Devine, that I haven't eaten a chocolate in fifteen years? I pay national insurance contributions too, and I don't get a No Claims Bonus for never needing a doctor. I keep myself fit, but you, you're just one self-inflicted wound after another. How many babies was it, five, all on the NHS?

None of those doctors out there smoke, or eat chocolate, or chips. They have to keep themselves fit, so they can cut open unhealthy old scumbags like you. Do you know what that's like, Mrs Devine, lifting up the blubber and laying it on one side to get at the poor little heart that split itself trying to keep your tub of lard on the road? We patch you up now and out you go to the nearest chippie to celebrate. You think your grandchildren would miss you, Mrs Devine? They will miss the sweets, that's what they will miss. Cupboard love. Turning them into grey lumps like yourself, weren't you Mrs Devine? Mrs Devine?

Oh, Sister, you'd better check Mrs Devine, she's gone very quiet.

Would you let Dr Darling know that he will be free after all. Tee off at 8. Ciao. Sister, you look peaky, you should take up golf.'

MICK JAGGER

I DON'T KNOW, ASK BILL

(Extract from Mick Somebody's autobiography)

In 1979 Mick Jagger was given a £1,000,000 advance for his autobiography. Eight months of painstaking research followed at the end of which he still didn't quite know what an autobiography was. Ronnie (Wood) thought it might be 'a kinda vegetable or somethin', like a courgette only longer'. Keef (Richards) didn't know either but said he'd like to try it 'like if you can get some, Mick'. Jagger was astonished when Bill (Wyman) told him it was a book, and not just any book: a book that Jagger himself would have to write. Bill unfortunately didn't know what the book was supposed to be about. Seizing on the word 'auto' Jagger wrote 150 pages on 'The History of the British Motor Car'.

As the headlines said at the time 'Jagger's Publishers Far From Satisfied' and it was the senior partner, Ernest Satisfied, that took him aside and broke the news. Jagger was stunned: the last definite memory he could identify was shaking hands with Mr Satisfied that morning.

Below is an exclusive extract from Mr Jagger's soon-to-be-published book . . . well short story really . . . OK, OK . . . Mr Jagger's soon-to-be-published pamphlet.

Yeh like it was eh back then and eh Keef came in and said like we're a band now and I like said what are we called then Keef and like he said well we're always gonna be on the road like we'll never stop like moving so let's call ourselves Dozy Beaky Micky Keef and Titch and like we did and then man Titch died and we got this guy Martin Luther King like to take over but then he forgot to get up one morning and that was Martin so we got this cat Kennedy but he went to Chappaquiddick who were like a three piece modern jazz combo and then Keef said Hey Mick try this stuff and like then I got the bus here this morning.

Below is the text of a recent interview with Jagger conducted by the NME journalist Etonboy Bedsit.

BEDSIT: Mick, what do you say to people who accuse you of having forgotten the last twenty years of your life?

JAGGER: Who's Mick?

BILLY CONNOLLY & PRINCE ANDREW

'Och, there's no' a lot in common 'tween us at first glance. I like fartin' and belchin' and makin' jokes about willies, while he has a taste for the high-life — polo and glasses of bubbly and mixin' with toffs' says H.R.H. Prince Andrew when asked to explain his friendship with Scottish comedian Billy Connolly.

Many on the Alternative Comedy circuit complain that Connolly has deserted his roots to become a court jester to the Royal Family, but nothing could be further from the truth. Born William Archibald Connolly in Gloucestershire, he was the son of a prominent solicitor and, following his education at The Dragon School and Harrow and after a short but successful stint at Sandhurst, Connolly decided that his future lay not in the law but in comedy.

Graduating from RADA with a degree in Glaswegian dialect, Connolly grew a beard, allowed his hair to become ragged and made his name cracking jokes about vomiting and copulating to young and predominantly drunken audiences.

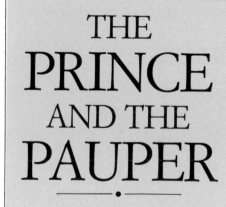

THE PRINCE AND THE PAUPER

Prince Andrew comes from an entirely different background. The only adopted child of H.M. The Queen, he is the son of a Gorbals topless dancer and a person or persons unknown. His assimilation into an environment so unlike that into which he was born has been noticeably successful. Only for his marriage to Sarah Ferguson has he returned to his roots: her great-grand-father, 'Colonel' Reggie Ferguson, is a bookie's stringer who still works the Don-caster circuit.

Connolly and his Roedean-educated wife Pamela will be representing their close friends The Duke and Duchess of York at the traditional Royal Family get-together at Balmoral this Christmas. 'They blend in perfectly, and William always makes Philip chuckle with his after-dinner impressions of an uncouth nouveau-riche social-climbing Scottish drunk' says a close friend of the family.

Meanwhile, the Yorks will be taking a break from their strenuous Royal impersonations to return to their first love — showbiz. Fergie will be appearing for a limited season with 'The Roly-Polys' song and dance troupe on The Pier, East-bourne, and hubby Andy will be joining Stuart Hall and friends for Radio 2's Boxing Day special, 'A Right Roy-Hall Christmas!'

P. W. BOTHA

Mr Botha is a very strange man. His private life is probably exemplary and he certainly goes to Church every Sunday and for all I know he says his prayers every night and regularly reads the Bible in bed. Having said that, and I'm not one for running anyone down unnecessarily, I have probably said all that there is good to say about Botha. Perhaps he is kind to cats as well. One's got to be fair. All right, cats and dogs. The trouble comes when we examine his public life. Now I am not privy to Mr Botha's prayers but, if his public behaviour is anything to go by, he must spend a good deal of his kneeling time asking The Almighty why He invented Blacks and what is the best way of getting rid of them. In the past, of course, Blacks were necessary to keep the South African economy running, and to keep them out of sight and preferably out of mind. Apartheid was created with Separate Areas and Influx Control and so on. But the problem with Apartheid is that it hasn't worked. Blacks actually insisted on learning to read and wholly unnecessary things like that. They simply wouldn't stay in their place. Then they started asking for votes and a share in the government. Incredible. Worse still they objected to being half-starved and beaten by the police and arrested for just being black. By the time Botha came to power it was very difficult to know what to do. All the colonial powers had chickened out of Africa and a fine old mess they'd left behind them. I don't know what advice God gave Botha but it can't have been very good. Everything he does seems to go wrong. He has the police shoot black students; he arrests thousands of children and gives them electric shock treatment and a good sjamboking, but it doesn't stop them. They go and take it out on 'good kaffirs', who do what the white man says, by filling perfectly good tyres (for black drivers anyhow) with very valuable petrol and stick this round the good kaffir's neck and light it. Well, Botha doesn't mind Blacks killing Blacks, even 'good' ones (the old adage about the only good one being a dead one still applies in South Africa) but that sort of thing can spread to Whites. He doesn't like Blacks going on strike either. And he particularly doesn't like them fighting back with guns and mines. But, if there is one thing he abominates, it is the ANC and the ANC refuses to go away. It grows stronger every day. I feel sorry for Mr Botha. He knows he's a loser and it must make him wonder what he's going to do with his nuclear weapons and nerve gas and all those tanks. Of course, if only Mrs Thatcher and dear old Ronnie would give him the say-so, he'd turn Soweto into a genuine gulag. I suspect he must think about the Shah of Iran and what happened to him. It's not much help having God on your side when you can't deal with Blacks as you wish. It's downright unfair.

BOTHA'S LITTLE BLOODBATH

MIKE TYSON AND FRANK BRUNO

SMOKIN' ST. BRUNO
CHAMP TYSON A SAD ONE-PUNCH WONDER

Hail the Hero! Sheer British skill and guts made last night's Wembley title clash one of the most heroically memorable in all the long annals of the richest prize in sport.

Although Britain's gallant and ever fearsome Frank failed to snatch the verdict over the American journeyman-champ, the self-styled Typhoon 'pigeonhead' Tyson, it was bombing, battling Bruno who won the hearts and minds of the nation. Raw, red courage was the name of this epic challenge. No Briton has made me prouder to be British. Unfurl those flags this morning!

For a champion, Tyson was frankly a flop, a woeful, one-punch wonder – and who could blame the vast and patriotic Wembley crowd displaying their disappointment with the Cuban referee's decision after just 23½ seconds of the contest, including the count which was, by my watch, picked up rather late by the confused, Spanish-speaking official.

A number of seats were soon turned to matchwood by exuberant British ringsiders, but I can report that not a single splinter ruffled the feathers of the so-called lucky mascot the champion sports on his close-cropped head – a bird that allegedly befriended him during his self-confessed 'hoodlum' days in Harlem.

But Percy the Pigeon had looked distinctly apprehensive during the fight – and no wonder, for Tyson needed all the fortune that was going to weather Bruno's magnificent opening onslaught. Razor-sharp and honed to a T, the superbly fit British boy towered over the American, who carried rolls of flab round his neck and shoulders as obvious testament to his lack of dedicated gymwork.

There was no way Tyson had trained to last the full 15.

ROUND ONE Bruno moved out smoothly at the bell, looking to finish it fast. His venomous first attack, a subtle, jerking feint with his left jab, was reminiscent of the opening moves which, in the past year, have so cruelly disposed of such top-flight warriors as the massive Austrian rock-lifter and yodeller, Gertan Daisi; the dangerous Portuguese 'man o'war' and sardine fisherman, Olivia Oilio; and the feared Juan Lee Ming, the deadly Puerto Rican part-time newsreader and taxi driver they call 'The Cobra'.

As Bruno's legendary piledriver homed in on its target, Tyson stuck out a limp, despairing fist. There was no power in it, but it slightly unbalanced the British and Empire champion and he appeared to slip on some canvas resin that had, disgracefully, been left in Tyson's corner. It was definitely a slip, but surprisingly the referee, obviously panicking, took up the count. Bruno was certainly not hurt, for I distinctly saw him smile the contented smile of a baby as he so slowly sank to the floor.

But, glory, glory, it was an unforgettable challenge – and when the ambulancemen had revived him exactly, by my watch, four hours and thirty-six minutes later at his traditional post-fight celebration at Luigi's, 227a Canning Town Road, Bruno told me, 'It's all part of my learning process; time is on my side, like I'm not 38 till November; I take each fight as it comes; everything I do is part of my education in ringcraft. Yes, if Terry can fix up the money right, like of course I demand a return.'

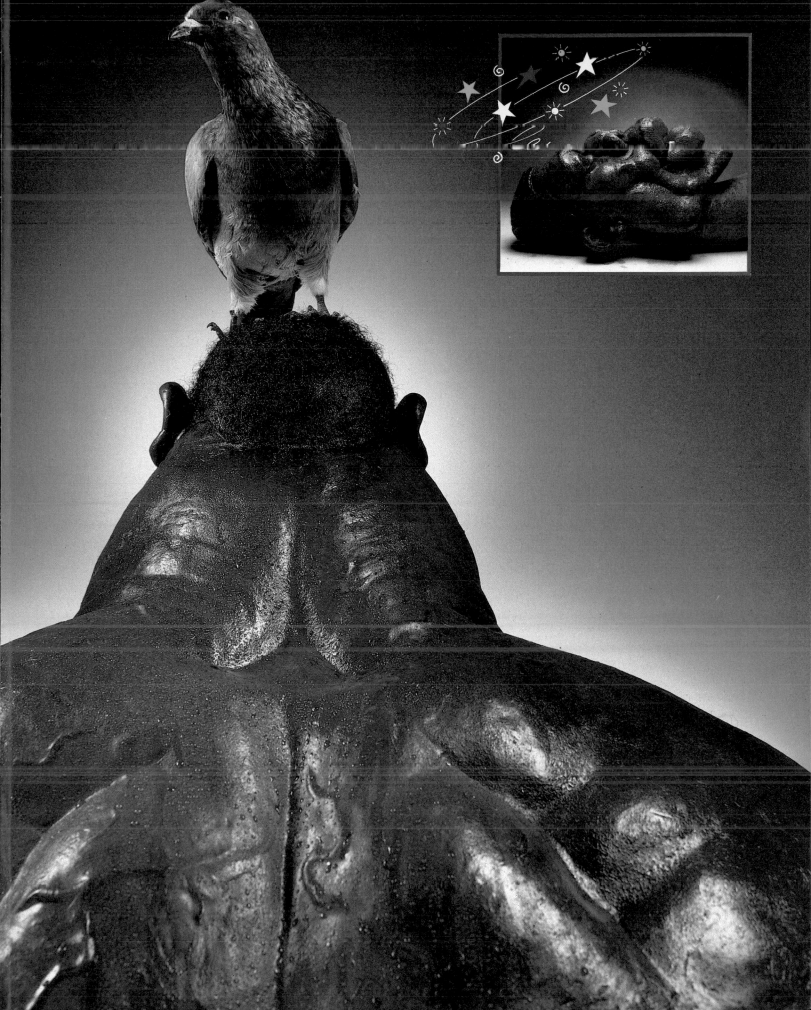

Dedicated to Francis Wyndham – the writer's friend.

Design by Shape of Things, London EC1

Thanks to Alice Cooper, Alex Evans, Matthew Evans, Clive Frampton, Charlie Gillat, Simon Inglis, Zoltan Marfy, Nicholas Wapshott and the Workshop Team: Jolly Aviary, Pablo Bach, Stephen Bendelack, Jeffrey Fineburg, Jackie Hallatt, Julien Short, David Stoten, Tim Watts, and the Moldies.

John Lawrence Jones was assisted by Sophie Kelly, Marco and Julie-Anne.

Typeset by Span Graphics Ltd, London EC1
Printed and bound in Great Britain by
McCorquodale Varnicoat Ltd, Pershore
Reproduced by Alpha Reprographic, Perivale

First published in 1987 by Century Hutchinson Ltd,
Brookmount House, 62-65 Chandos Place, Covent Garden,
London WC2N 4NW

Century Hutchinson Australia Pty Ltd,
PO Box 496, 16-22 Church Street, Hawthorn, Victoria 3122,
Australia

Century Hutchinson New Zealand Ltd,
PO Box 40-086, Glenfield, Auckland 10,
New Zealand

Century Hutchinson South Africa Pty Ltd,
PO Box 337, Bergvlei, 2012 South Africa

ISBN 0 7126 1758 2